CU00843119

Contents

Introduction

For the past twenty years, I have been writing historical fiction as a hobby, something I did in my spare time. Over the course of about fifteen years, I managed to complete a historical novel. My novel took several forms, shape-shifting from a third person narrative, to a first, and then back to a third again. Many scenes were written, edited, redrafted, deleted, restored and re-edited. I performed a major edit again when I was preparing the manuscript for publication. All in all, I made a long process significantly longer.

Whilst writing, I devoured 'How To' books, hoping to find, if not a magical formula, then at least some guidance on how to write historical fiction. In comparison to other genres, there weren't that many books dedicated solely to historical fiction, and many of those available spent too many pages giving examples of great historical fiction and the reasons for wanting to write it before getting down to the nitty gritty.

Last year, spurred on by the self-publishing revolution, I decided to dust off my finished manuscript and create an eBook. I did not harbour great hopes of huge sales, nor did I have a burning desire to see my name in print. My main reason for self-publishing was that I had recently become self-employed as a Copywriter and Virtual Assistant, and eBook creation was one of the services I wanted to offer. I didn't feel that I could offer eBook creation to other people if I hadn't done it for myself. So, 2013 saw my novel, '*The Queen's Favourite*', published on

Amazon as a Kindle eBook and Print on Demand paperback.

Now I want to share some of the things I learned while writing my historical fiction novel. Some of the methods discussed in this guide will be relevant to writing all types of fiction, not just historical. As I am a Brit, and British history is what I know about and enjoy, this guide refers exclusively to British history, but the principles will naturally apply to all countries.

It is beyond the scope of this guide to tell you how to format your manuscript, approach an agent or self-publish. I just want to help you get your historical novel written.

So, shall we make a start?

CHAPTER ONE - Where to start

First things first

I'm assuming that since you're reading this book, you have an interest in writing your own historical fiction. I'm going to make some other assumptions. That you love history, but are not necessarily a scholar or academic. That you love to read fiction. That your favourite reading material is therefore a genre that blends the two - historical fiction. And that lastly, you have a talent for writing, and you have a story you want to tell.

Define your genre

But there isn't just one type of historical fiction, there are several, and before you start, you need to define which type you are going to write.

Let's take the all-encompassing genre of Historical Fiction and define it. Historical fiction is a brand of fiction that is set (almost) exclusively in the past, and may take as main or secondary characters real historical figures, such as Elizabeth I or Marie Antoinette, and will use recorded historical events as a main plot or subplot. Some examples of these types of historical fiction novels that are sitting on my bookshelves are -

I Claudius by Robert Graves
Wolf Hall by Hilary Mantel
The Memoirs of Cleopatra by Margaret George
Katherine by Anya Seton

Now, let me just justify that '(almost)' for a moment. There are historical novels that use a device known as a 'time slip', where two time-frames are involved, the past and the present. Barbara Erskine, for example, often writes these types of novels. Her main characters usually inhabit the present day, but something happens to them, whether it be drug-induced or otherwise, that transports them, either physically or mentally, back to the past, and they experience events as if they were actually there. Some examples of these types of time slip novels are -

Lady of Hay by Barbara Erskine
The House on the Strand by Daphne du Maurier
Labyrinth by Kate Mosse

There is also Historical Romance, which has the settings and backdrops of historical fiction, but has romance at its heart and as its main plot and theme. These types of books are popular with publishers such as Mills and Boon, who have great success with their Regency romances. Some examples of these types of novels are -

From Ruins to Riches by Louise Allen
The Virgin Courtesan by Michelle Kelly
Duke of Deception by Stephie Smith

And then there are Historical Mysteries. This is where a main character has a puzzle to solve, perhaps a real historical mystery, and goes in search of the truth, encountering danger at every turn. These are similar in concept to modern thrillers, but have constraints self-imposed on them by the nature of the times in which they are set. Some examples of these novels are -

Dissolution by C.J. Sansom
The Name of the Rose by Umberto Eco
The Silver Pigs by Lindsey Davies

Of course, any genre of novel may contain elements of some or all of these, but if you are looking to the future and are going to try to get a traditional publisher to take you on, or even self-publish, it will be very helpful if your historical novel fits into one of these sub-categories.

Get reading

One thing a writer should be is a reader. To understand historical fiction well enough to be able to write it, you need to read plenty of published historical fiction novels. Pick up a popular historical fiction novel, one that has garnered praise and good reviews, or even one that you have particularly enjoyed, and go through it, analysing the text.

How does it open, with a tease or a bang? Is it written in the first or third person? How much historical detail is written into the scenes? Does each chapter end with a hook, a cliff-hanger? Is the protagonist male or female? Is the main focus on history or is it there more as a backdrop? What is the prevalent theme? What is the dialogue to prose ratio?

These are the sort of questions you should be asking as you read. And as you try to pin down the elements that make the novel work, remember to make notes.

CHAPTER TWO - Getting ideas

It may be that you want to write a historical novel, but don't have an idea for one. So, how do you go about getting an idea, or two, or dozens?

Ask any writer where he or she gets their ideas from, and, unless they are being really polite, your question will be answered with a groan. Who can say where ideas come from? They just pop into the brain, and either germinate and bear fruit, or wither and die.

If you haven't got an idea for a story, then you're going to have to read history books, old newspapers, watch period dramas, in fact, immerse yourself in history to spark an idea. Or you could try reading the newspaper and consider how some of the news stories would have happened in the past. How would a bank robbery be carried out in the nineteenth century? What religious questions were being asked in Charles II's time? How was terrorism combated in the early twentieth century? One thing you need to be certain of is that there is a sound reason for placing your story in a historical context. This means making sure your story can only be told properly by its being set in the past.

Hopefully though you already have an idea. Perhaps your story is based on a real historical figure, in which case your plot is pretty much already worked out for you. This is a boon for the beginning writer, as the most important events in your story will come from your main character's life. Many historical fiction novels, my own included, have a true historical figure as their lead. Some follow a character from their birth to their death, while others focus on a single, defining event in their life.

Almost all historical fiction will contain some real people, even if they just pass through or get a name check in one scene. A way of making your novel a little bit different is to create an original character who witnesses the true historical events and interacts with the historical figure. Examples of this type of novel include -

The Warlord Chronicles by Bernard Cornwell - deals with the story of King Arthur, but told by a soldier who served with him.

Girl with a Pearl Earring by Tracy Chevalier - features real historical figure Johannes Vermeer, but told from the viewpoint of the sitter in one of his paintings.

Portrait of an Unknown Woman by Vanora Bennett - a Tudor novel about Sir Thomas More told by a little known member of his adopted family.

History is getting smaller. For hundreds of years, historians considered only the wide canvas, the big names, kings and queens, revolutionaries and rebels. In the last decade or so, interest has moved to micro-history, focusing on a much smaller aspect of history, so we now have history books such as *Cod: A Biography Of The Fish That Changed The World* by Mark Kurlansky, and *Consider the Fork: A History of How We Cook and Eat* by Bee Wilson. We can adapt this way of looking at history to historical fiction and use it to shine new light on previously little known topics. Examples of this type of historical fiction novel include -

Tipping the Velvet by Sarah Waters - bringing the previously little-known world of Victorian lesbianism to a mass audience

Remarkable Creatures by Tracy Chevalier - telling the story of fossil hunting at Lyme Regis featuring real historical figures

And then you could always use another author's fictional character, such as Sherlock Holmes, Mr Darcy, Jane Eyre or Macbeth. Your novel could be a prequel, starting before readers first met the character, or sequels, continuing their story where the original author left off. Some readers, known as purists, hate this, because of how an author treats their favourite character, making them act or giving them personality traits that are not in line with the original creation. Other readers love it, enjoying the further adventures of characters they can't get enough of. Examples of these types of novel include -

The Last Sherlock Holmes Story by Michael Dibdin
Mrs de Winter by Susan Hill
Wide Sargasso Sea by Jean Rhys

Writing to order

You may be looking at the long term and thinking that a particular period of history sells well in terms of fiction at the moment, so that is the period in which you are going to set your story.

This means you will be following a trend, and trends come and go. By the time you have finished your novel, the trend may have passed. For example, the Tudor era provides plenty of scope and drama for historical fiction, and the market could be said to have become saturated with fiction set in this period. Speaking purely as a reader who loves the Tudor period, I confess I have grown a little tired of novels about Henry VIII, Elizabeth I and other big names of the era because they all seem to tell the same story.

Ah, but I hear you say, your own novel, *The Queen's Favourite*, is set in the Tudor era and features Elizabeth I. Why was it all right for you to write and publish yet another Tudor novel?

I agree, but I have two arguments that I offer in defence.

When I first started writing my novel, back in 1995, historical fiction had not really taken off in the way it since has. For example, Philippa Gregory had yet to publish her massively successful *The Other Boleyn Girl,* and Hilary Mantel's award-winning Thomas Cromwell trilogy, beginning with *Wolf Hall,* was a long way off.

Secondly, it was the character of Robert Dudley that had captivated me, not the potential publishing rewards, as being published was an extremely distant hope at the time. I just wanted to write about *him*, from his perspective rather than Elizabeth's.

The Wars of the Roses era has now become a popular period to set novels in, due I suspect in no small part to Philippa Gregory. Maybe the trend after that will be the Civil War, or the Conquest. Who can say? Don't try and move with the times.

Ultimately, you have to write the story you want to write, and if you are intent on writing a novel that is set in an already extremely popular period, then try to use either less well-known historical figures, or create an original character, who could be a servant, an official, a distant relative, or an enemy.

Remember, some readers will be reading your book to gain an entry-level insight into the period, whilst others will already be very familiar with the era. Try to give this latter group a different perspective on a period they think they know well.

CHAPTER THREE - Doing your homework

So you have your story idea and your main characters, but you need to know more about the world in which they lived.

When should you begin your research? My answer is as early as you can.

Historical fiction is, in many ways, a far more demanding genre than other types of fiction. You as the writer have to learn what your characters' world was like if you are going to convince your readers. Research by reading about your chosen period and make copious notes as you go.

Books are your most obvious resources for research, and you should always try to get hold of the latest biographies and histories, rather than books written and published fifty years ago or more. They will include the latest discoveries and theories, and are far more likely to focus on personalities rather than dates and events, which should help you to understand and flesh out your characters.

With historical biographies of your main character, make detailed notes of every event of importance in their lives - what happened, how they acted, who was with them, what they said, and what contemporary accounts reported. These could help you to create scenes, find motivations for your characters and even give you lines for your dialogue.

Use social histories to find out about the world your characters inhabited. Your research may include some of the following:

Currency
Social divisions
Fashion
Forms of address
Medicine
Law
Entertainments and amusements
Travelling
Health and hygiene
When, what and how they ate
Etiquette and manners
Road systems
Architecture
Interior decoration
Gardens and parks
Hunting
National attitudes
Sex
Marriage and children
Social customs
Religion
Holidays and holy days
Education
Crime and punishment
Witchcraft and magic
Uniforms
Farming

For the novice writer, I would advise against trying to conduct your own research using primary and original documents. Leave this type of research to scholars and historians, who have experience in contacting libraries and museums to arrange viewings of the original documents.

Use the Internet for research, but exercise caution when doing so. Not everyone who writes on the Internet is careful about facts. Always corroborate dates and other checkable facts by cross-referencing them with at least two other sources.

Be aware that your research will probably continue even while you write your book, but be careful to not over-research at the beginning of your writing journey. History books can be fascinating and you might be tempted to read everything you can get your hands on. Yes, you'll learn a lot, but much of what you learn will not end up in your story. Focus your research. As you work your way through your first draft, you'll probably suddenly realise you have a gap in your knowledge. This is the time to go and find out about it. Don't become so bogged down with facts and figures that you never get down to writing.

When it comes to the writing, don't show off all of your research by including lengthy, textbook-like paragraphs of explanation in your story. It's a novel you are writing after all, not a history book.

Lastly, be aware that despite all your research, you will still get things wrong. All writers have to accept this. That's why you may have seen disclaimers at the start of books saying things like 'Any mistakes in this work are my own'. Just don't make your mistakes big ones, like having characters eat potatoes in the Dark Ages or smoking a cigarette in the twelfth century.

Giving them a sense of place

If your characters were real people, then you are probably going to have them occupy real places too. In the UK, there are plenty of historic buildings still standing which you can visit to get a sense of the architecture, decoration and layout of houses for your time period.

Invaluable resources for this type of research are The National Trust and English Heritage. The National Trust generally maintain furnished places, and they usually date from around the Early Modern period onwards, whereas English Heritage mainly have buildings and ruins that are earlier. These types of sites can be extremely evocative, especially if you visit on a day when there aren't many people around. You may need a bit of imagination to see how they would have looked in your story's time period, but that shouldn't be too difficult. You're a writer - imagination is your stock in trade.

Sometimes, stately homes are furnished and set out how they looked during a certain period of their history. Chartwell, Sir Winston Churchill's country residence, for example, has the dining room and study set out as it was when he lived there. Set pieces like this can be extremely helpful for understanding a real-life character and helps to root their life in the landscape. It can also give you incredible detail for the descriptive passages of your book.

Take a notebook and a camera with you when you visit a stately home or other location. Make notes and take plenty of pictures, both of the house and gardens, and if you are allowed, of items inside the house.

Off-topic tip - With your camera, try to take atmospheric and artistic shots of the buildings and grounds. If you are planning to self-publish and design your own book cover, you may find that one of these photographs will be suitable for it.

A short list of some popular social histories to aid your research:

The Time Traveller's Guide to Medieval England - Ian Mortimer

The Time Traveller's Guide to Elizabethan England - Ian Mortimer

Elizabeth's London: Everyday Life in Elizabethan London - Liza Picard

Dr Johnson's London: Everyday Life in London in the Mid-18th Century - Liza Picard

Restoration London: Everyday Life in the 1660s - Liza Picard

Victorian London: The Life of a City 1840-1870 - Liza Picard

The Victorian City: Everyday Life in Dickens' London - Judith Flanders

The Victorian House: Domestic Life from Childbirth to Deathbed - Judith Flanders

Consuming Passions: Leisure and Pleasure in Victorian Britain - Judith Flanders

How to be a Victorian - Ruth Goodman

Pepys London: Everyday Life in London 1650 - 1703 - Stephen Porter

London in the Eighteenth Century: A Great and Monstrous Thing - Jerry White

A Brief History of Life in the Middle Ages - Martyn Whittock

A Brief History of the Wars of the Roses - Desmond Seward

A Brief History of the English Civil Wars - John Miller

A trawl on Amazon or other online bookshops will throw up a whole host of entry-level history books for you to begin your research.

However, I heartily recommend that once you have identified the books which will be of most use, you order them from your local library. If you are doing your research properly, you will refer to several history books, which if bought would cost you a small fortune. You may only be dipping in and out of them and reading sections relevant to your novel, so why spend all that money?

Ordering books from the library is free and you can often renew books up to twelve times. That could equate to months of ownership, plenty of time to find what you want in them. If you do have to give them back before you are finished with them, you can always re-order. Not only will you be keeping your bank balance healthy, but you'll be helping to keep the library open too.

By the way, it is a good idea to keep a list of the books you use in your research, in case you want to create a bibliography at the end of your novel.

Helpful Links

This page is a very selective list of links that I have come across related to writing historical fiction and which may be of use to you in your research.

It is by no means exhaustive, and a quick trawl of the Internet will throw up literally hundreds more.

Websites come and go, and while these links were all active at the time of writing, they may occasionally break.

Visiting:

English Heritage
http://www.english-heritage.org.uk/

National Trust
https://www.nationaltrust.org.uk/

National Gallery
http://www.nationalgallery.org.uk/

National Portrait Gallery
http://www.npg.org.uk/

Tate Britain
http://www.tate.org.uk

The Wallace Collection
http://www.wallacecollection.org

The Royal Academy of Arts
http://www.royalacademy.org.uk

Victoria and Albert Museum
http://www.vam.ac.uk/

British Museum
http://www.britishmuseum.org/

Museum of London
http://www.museumoflondon.org.uk/

British Library
http://www.bl.uk/

Geffrye Museum
http://www.geffrye-museum.org.uk

Imperial War Museum
http://www.iwm.org.uk

National Maritime Museum
http://www.nmm.ac.uk

Science Museum
http://www.sciencemuseum.org.uk

Online Resources:

Luminarium: Anthology of English Literature
http://www.luminarium.org/

The Victorian Web
http://www.victorianweb.org/

The Dictionary of Victorian London
http://www.victorianlondon.org/

Historical Novel Society
http://historicalnovelsociety.org/

British History Online: Primary and Secondary
Sources for Medieval & Modern History of Britain
http://www.british-history.ac.uk/

Regency era timeline
http://candicehern.com/regency-world/regency-
timeline/

Measuring Worth
http://www.measuringworth.com/ppoweruk/

Old Bailey Online
http://www.oldbaileyonline.org/

Food timeline
http://www.foodtimeline.org/

Regency lexicon
http://www.regencyassemblypress.com/Regency_Lex
icon.html

Fashion Era
http://www.fashion-era.com/

Correct forms of address
http://www.debretts.com/forms-address

All about surnames
http://surname.sofeminine.co.uk/w/surnames/uk.html

British Newspaper Archive
http://www.britishnewspaperarchive.co.uk/

The National Archives
http://www.nationalarchives.gov.uk/

Writing Opportunities:

Mills and Boon Historical Romance
http://www.millsandboon.co.uk/How-to-write-historical-romance

Harlequin Historical Romance
http://www.harlequin.com/articlepage.html?articleId=538&chapter=0

National Novel Writing Month
http://nanowrimo.org/

Historical Novel Society
http://historicalnovelsociety.org/

CHAPTER FOUR - The business of writing

Type of narration

One big decision to make before you begin writing is to decide which form of narration you will be using.

The choices are:

1st person narration - Where the story reads as written by a character, and they address themselves as 'I'.

2nd person narration - Where the story is written by a character or narrator, and 'You' is used.

3rd person narration - Where the story is written from an omniscient viewpoint, and people are addressed as 'he', 'she', 'they', 'them'.

Which one is right for you?

First person narration

First person narration is generally perceived as an easy way for the writer to allow a reader into the mind of the main character. A reader's immersion in their world is immediate, and the writer need only imagine how the character is feeling and what they are thinking to let the words flow.

Despite these seeming advantages, there are limits to this form of narration. The main character's is the only viewpoint, so all the action has to come from them. For example, if they do not witness a battle, they cannot therefore describe it in detail. They cannot know the thoughts of the other characters; they can only assume things from the actions those characters make.

There are ways around this, however. It is possible to have multiple viewpoints in the first person by the author adopting an epistolary style novel. This means writing the novel using diaries and letters. So one character can receive a letter from another character, and by this means, an author can describe an event not specifically witnessed by the main character. However, the shifting of viewpoint can become confusing for a reader if it is not properly handled.

For some reason, historical fiction is particularly fond of first person narration, perhaps more so than other genres. It obviously works well, just be aware of its limitations.

Second person narration

Whilst it is common for this type of non-fiction book, second person narration is rare in most novels, not just historical fiction. Second person narration, by virtue of addressing 'you', involves its reader directly and admittedly, it is how most of us talk, "you know what I mean?"

To my mind however, it has a presumptuous, accusative tone, and I would notice the use of 'you' so much that it would distract me from the story I'm trying to get engaged in. Saying that, as it is used so infrequently, it is one way of getting your story noticed, but it is probably best avoided for the novice.

Third person narration

Third person narration is the most common form of narration, and for the beginner, the easiest to handle. A story narrated in the third person has a god-like figure explaining what is going on. They see everything and they know everything.

This type of narration has its pitfalls too, however. Any scene in this style needs to be written from only one point of view at any one time. For example, if you start a scene off with Mr Darcy, then everything in that scene needs to be written from his point of view (POV) - what he sees, what he says, what he thinks - even when Elizabeth Bennett wanders into the scene and starts up a conversation with him.

Characters

Visualising your characters

If you are like me, your idea for a story starts with a character. Perhaps you have a vivid picture of what he or she looks like, how they talk and how they move. But if all you have are a few personality traits, then you might need a little help to really 'see' your character.

The following method works for me. I visualise an actor or actress who would play my character were my novel ever turned into a visual medium, such as a TV series or film.

Get hold of a photograph of that actor, and print it off in colour. Stick it to your wall or wherever you write. You now have a face for your character. You might want to change that face; make the eyes blue instead of brown, hair black instead of blond, add a scar, or pock marks, or whatever. You even have a sense of how they sound, if their voice is deep or high, gravelly or smooth.

When you look at this picture, try not to see the actor, see your character instead.

Naming your characters

Names, just like clothes and hairstyles, have fashions. It is essential that you give your characters names that fit with their times. I know you're not daft, and you know that giving your 14th century heroine the name 'Kylie' would be completely anachronistic, but there are other names that sound old but may not be, and vice versa. Phoebe, for example, sounds quite modern but actually hails from Ancient Greek mythology. And Victoria only became a popular girls name when Queen Victoria came to the throne - it was practically unheard of in England before then.

You can source names from contemporary documents, or you can go through baby name books. Often these type of books will also have the meaning of a name, which can be a real help when trying to find a name that suits your character. Even better if the name is accompanied by a date and place of origin so that you can be sure of its authenticity. As an alternative to researching names, many writing software packages will have an in-built Name Generator to come up with names for you. Some of these however, will be truly bizarre.

It was often fashionable, and politic, to name babies after the king or queen, so if your historical novel is set in a monarch's court, such as Elizabeth I, it would be quite usual to have a number of Elizabeth's around. However, in fiction it is not a good idea to have too many character names that all begin with the same letter or sound too similar, as it will become confusing for the reader. In my novel, *The Queen's Favourite*, there were several historical characters that were called Edward, Thomas and Robert. As these were real, recognisable people, it was not possible to change their names, so I called them by their surnames or titles to differentiate between them.

They weren't born yesterday

Well, all right, they may have been, in your head, but they still need a history to be convincing on the page. We as people are the sum of our experiences. So are your characters.

You need to create a background or backstory for them. You need to know when they were born, the names of their parents, brothers and sisters, where they went to school, what accidents they had, who influenced them and so on. You need to know what they like and dislike, what their favourite books are, what music they like to listen to, what food and drink they enjoy.

Much of the background you create for your character will not be used in your novel, but it is necessary for you to know it. Only by understanding your character's history will you know why he acts the way he does, says the things he says, and feels the things he feels. All of these unique things will help you to create a believable character, and may even take your plot down roads you hadn't considered going.

There are low-tech and high-tech ways of creating character backgrounds. Low-tech can be as basic as creating a CV or filling in a template, such as the one which can be found on my website here: http://bit.ly/1kLWL8R .

High tech ways will include the use of special, dedicated software, which will ask you all the right questions and store your answers.

Use whatever works best for you.

The tricky business of planning

Apparently there are two types of writers; those who plan their stories and those who don't.

Most writers will be a bit of both, but a workable plot is essential to a successful novel, so for the novice, an outline is a good tool to make use of. Some experienced writers who use an outline call this part of the writing process the most difficult to do, and it is easy to understand why.

Writing an outline means planning out every significant stage of your story, so that you have a beginning where the conflict is introduced, a middle where it reaches a crisis point, and an ending or denouement where the conflict is resolved.

You may feel you have a problem here. You know the beginning of your story and how it will end, but you don't yet know how your characters are going to get from one to the other. The middle part of a novel is notoriously the most difficult to get right. Without knowing the outline of your novel, chances are you will get a few chapters in and find yourself floundering for what to write next. Or you may end up writing your characters into a corner with no means of escape. You are going to need an outline.

An outline can be as simple as a sheet of paper, or as complex as a small booklet worth of well-planned scenes and notes. I have a simple three act outline available for download on my website here: http://bit.ly/1kLWL8R.

Or you can take a sheet of A4 paper, number sequentially in the margin, and write a one-line scene synopsis against each number. If you don't know every single scene, don't panic, simply miss out that line. Write in what you do know, leave out what you don't.

You can also use postcards or similar sized cards, which can then be shuffled around until you have the plot line that works best.

Think of the outline as a road map for your novel. As you write, you may find yourself thinking of 'routes' that you hadn't considered before and end up going 'off-piste' which can be very exciting. I'm mixing my metaphors here, but you get the idea.

An outline will keep your writing on track and make that first draft much more achievable.

The title

Don't waste time trying to think up a good title before you begin writing. If you have one in mind before you start, all well and good. If you don't and feel you need a title and '*Work in Progress*' won't do, then think of a word, phrase or sentence that best describes your book. I had several titles for my first novel, from '*Robert Dudley, The Gypsy*', '*The Bear and Ragged Staff*', and '*Robert and Elizabeth*', before finally settling on its published title of '*The Queen's Favourite*'. It is quite likely that the title for your book will evolve naturally from your writing.

But you will need to come up with a title that does justice to your work once you have a finished manuscript. Try and find an original and inspiring title for your book, or better still, five original and inspiring titles. Show these five titles to your friends and family, and get their feedback on the ones they like and don't like, and do take note of their preferences. After all, they will represent your readers.

It can be a good idea to come up with a title that has more than one meaning to catch the interest of bookshelf browsers.

If you're writing a historical mystery, don't use a title that gives away the plot.

Different genres also have their own style of titles. For example, my title of *The Queen's Favourite* is unlikely to be mistaken for a modern spy story or psychological thriller.

If you can imply the past in your title, all the better for when it comes to marketing it.

To type or not to type?

How do you write? By downloading this eBook, I know you're computer savvy, which means that you may type straight onto a computer screen. Some authors find this way best, while other authors, such as Tracy Chevalier, prefer to write a first draft in longhand and then type up the second draft.

I suspect many authors do a bit of both. I know I don't always feel like working on the computer as I do enough of that during my working day as it is, and sometimes I just use a piece of paper and a pen to write. When I feel like it, I type up what I've written.

There is no right way. Just do whatever works best for you. The main thing is that you're continuing to write.

Off-topic tip. Sitting for long periods at a desk typing can have an extremely detrimental effect on the body. Ensure that your workspace is properly set up. The computer screen should ideally be at eye level, and the keyboard right in front of you. This means your elbows should be gently brushing the sides of your body, and form a right-angle from shoulder to hand. I have learned the hard way that this is the best typing position after years of having the keyboard at an arm's length from my body, resulting in daily neck, shoulder and arm aches.

Regarding equipment, because of the amount of typing I have to do, I have recently changed my standard mouse and keyboard for ergonomic ones, and I feel that they are better for me, though not everyone will find them so.

When we stare at screens, our blink rate reduces from about 22 blinks to 7 blinks per minute, and our eyes stop producing the necessary amount of lubricating fluid. This can result in dry eyes, which become itchy, red and sore. For this reason, I have also invested in a dictation software kit, where I speak into a headset microphone and the computer types my words, without me even needing to be directly in front of the screen. This is a great way to still work but have a break from typing and the computer.

Another piece of equipment to consider, and one that has been in the press quite a bit lately, is a standing desk. This is an ideal way to stay working yet avoid getting stuck in the same seated position for hours at a time.

Finally, take plenty of breaks away from the computer. Get out of the chair for fifteen minutes, have a walk around, make a cup of tea. Anything to stop you staring at the screen. Your body will thank you for it.

Filling the blank page

Now all you have to do is start writing, which may not be as easy as it sounds. Sometimes, actually writing is more frightening than not being able to write at all. Writing a first draft is the hardest thing to achieve and many writers put it off as long as possible.

I do think it is far better to just start writing in order to get something down on paper, or on screen. However, if you are one of these people who prefer to write using a definite structure, then it may be useful at this stage to plan your individual scenes. To help you do this, I have put a simple document on my website, which you can download for free and use. It uses the five senses to help you create a fully realised environment. The link is here: http://bit.ly/1kLWL8R .

Useful as this template may prove to be, (and I hope it is), if you have nothing written, there is nothing to improve upon. You can always save this template for the second draft.

Resist the impulse to edit on a daily basis. Write a scene and move on to the next. If you're stuck on what to write for the next scene, use your outline to move on to a scene that you are sure of. You'll move farther, faster, if you stop editing as you go. When you have a complete first draft, then you can go back and edit it.

My first novel took me so long to write because I would write a few pages at a time, edit, write a bit more, edit, and then edit again. I'm sure that if I had stopped my inner critic a lot earlier, the book would have been written in at least half the time. There's nothing wrong with wanting to make something good, but to keep going back over the previous day's work is a guaranteed way of ensuring the end of your book is a long way off.

CHAPTER FIVE - The nuts and bolts of Historical Fiction

Entering a lost world

The past is gone. All we have are books and pictures to tell us how things once were.

What we have to remember is that our perception of the past is coloured by our ideas of the present. Let me give you an example.

History is a brutal place. The Romans used to watch people die in gladiatorial games and think it fun; Elizabethans would watch a bear baiting and enjoy the bear and dogs tearing each other to pieces; even the Victorians used to enjoy a public hanging. We enlightened twenty-first century people think this kind of behaviour is despicable, horrific, sadistic, and yes, it is. But the point to remember is that it wouldn't have been to a Roman, an Elizabethan or a Victorian. And this is why historical fiction can sometimes be difficult to stomach and write convincingly.

A historical novel would not ring true with your readers if you were to have a main character who lectures his or her contemporaries on the barbaric nature of the bear baiting, and claim that the animal has rights too. A true Elizabethan would not understand this concept. They believed that there was a natural hierarchy to life, with Man at the top and animals at the bottom for humans to do with as they pleased. They even had a hierarchy for people;

noblemen were inherently better than yeoman, and so on.

But how to make a modern historical novel fit with its times and yet not disgust your readers? Perhaps you need a cock fight scene in your book, but you don't want your main character to enjoy it and thereby lose the sympathy of your readers. Maybe you can have him watch it and yet not show the enjoyment his fellow spectators display, or try and watch it, but have to turn his head away, prompting a contemptuous comment from a less squeamish secondary character. What you can't have is your main character jumping into the ring, setting the cocks free and threatening the owner with the RSPCA.

Remember, your job as a historical fiction writer is to expose history, not judge it.

Whilst it can be very tempting, especially if you are writing a Historical Romance, to make your characters wonderfully attractive, remember that the past would have been a very unclean place with poor sanitation, rudimentary open sewers and untreatable diseases. So it wouldn't ring true to give your characters minty fresh breath and gleaming white teeth, taking a wash every five minutes or enjoying perfect health throughout their life.

Keep in mind too that the past was a lot more religious than today. For the pagan Romans, practically every aspect of their day, whether it was trading, making a decision or sowing a field with corn, was governed by the gods. For Christians from the post-Roman era onwards, God was an ever-present entity, to be worshipped and feared in equal measure. Relics of saints were believed to have healing properties, and there were Saint Days and Holy Days. There was really no such thing as an atheist during these times, just different ways of worshipping, especially after the Reformation. People had an absolute belief in the Afterlife, and pre-Reformation, a certainty in Heaven, Hell and Purgatory. People were prepared to die in agony for their religious beliefs, so make sure you recognise this commitment to religion in your story.

There is another problem regarding attitudes and mind-sets. A leading character in a historical novel, whilst they have to be interesting, charismatic and clever, must not come across as too modern. It is no good having a female lead who is spirited, dismissive of rules and promiscuous, if the time in which she lives does not allow for these qualities. For example, a woman living before birth control could not have sex without worrying about becoming pregnant, contracting a sexual disease or damaging her reputation. Your readers will pick up on such an anachronistic character immediately and your story will lose its credibility.

Conversely, it is no good making your character completely of their time. Take the Victorian era as an example. Women were supposed to be meek and mild, submissive to their husbands, not permitted to voice any political opinions, or even have any opinions at all. Now, would you want to read about a character that is like this, or would you think she is unbelievably dull? I'm guessing the latter. So the trick is finding a middle ground, where the character has the mind-set of a Roman, an Elizabethan or Victorian, but manages to push against the constraints of their time.

Human nature doesn't change all that much; men and women five hundred years ago felt as we do today in that they loved, hated, got upset, got angry. It's just they had to deal with it in a different way. Women may have exercised their intelligence by being the power behind their husbands, for example, or dressed up as men to become highwaymen or pirates.

A lead in a modern historical novel needs to be of their time, and yet somehow ahead of it, staying true to the period by acknowledging its limits. Just make sure your main character is still interesting enough to be worth reading about.

Changing history

Shakespeare never let historical fact get in the way of a good story, and there's no reason why you need to either. History is there to be used as a framework, a backdrop to your story. If by keeping true to history means that you have to sacrifice a crucial piece of your plot, then it isn't worth it. If you think a particular factual historical scene doesn't have enough drama or conflict in it, invent some. Bring in another character to add some conflict and stir things up a bit. Allow yourself to deviate from history for the good of your story.

Be aware that this is not going to please all readers. Some readers are purists and do not like books to change history for the sake of drama. If you are going to deviate from historical fact and feel that you might be criticised for it or seem like you don't know what you're talking about, then include an Afterword in your novel, explaining what really happened in history, and a little explanation of why you changed it. This should satisfy your critics, and prove to your readers you made an informed and deliberate choice when writing your book.

Language

"Verily, forsooth, I wot not what you do. I prithee, come hither."

Can you imagine an entire novel written in this kind of pseudo-Shakespearean language, how tedious it would be? Whilst it would not be suitable to use modern words, phrases or rhythms of speech, such as 'okay', 'comfort zone', or 'ya think?' in your historical novel, using deliberately archaic language in order to establish a time period would be equally inappropriate.

The best way to get around this is to use modern language, but in such a way that it replicates the rhythm of speech in your chosen period. In some cases, etiquette may help you to emulate a way of speech. For example, a novel from mediaeval times with monarchs and nobles as characters will naturally involve quite a few instances of 'Your Majesty',

'Your Grace', and 'my lord', while a Regency novel will use titles, such as 'Mister', 'Lady' and 'Sir'.

Read some of your favourite historical fiction authors to see how they handle language. A very good example of how period-sounding dialogue can be used in a novel and not detract from the story is in C.J. Sansom's *Matthew Shardlake* books. Just have a look through one of these books to see how Mr Sansom uses 16th century language without making it sound like Shakespeare.

Slang can be a particularly effective way of not only defining a time, but also a class system. For example, during the flapper era of the 1920s, phrases such as 'It's just too, too sick-making', 'What ho!' or 'Very very' were used mostly by the Bright Young Things of the upper classes, rather than the working classes. To find out how people talked in the 19th and early 20th centuries, read novels from these times and analyse their language patterns.

Some might disagree with me on this point, but I think a few well chosen, archaic words dotted throughout your novel, especially in dialogue, can help to set the scene and time period. For example, there are a huge number of words in Samuel Johnson's dictionary that are no longer in use, or changed their meaning, such as a 'clapperdudgeon', who was a type of Elizabethan beggar, 'punk', which means a fan of a certain type of music or dress sense, but back in the Elizabethan era meant a whore, or 'gay', which now means homosexual, but once meant happy. The only caveat is that you can't just drop an archaic word into your prose without giving some explanation or making it clear what the word means.

Don't sprinkle such words around simply to prove that you know your historical period and show how clever you are. Make sure there is a good reason to include them.

Adding a bibliography

The list you made of the books you consulted during your research phase will form the basis of this page. Including a bibliography at the end of your novel is a good idea for two reasons.

1. It proves to your readers that you were serious about getting the historical context of your story right and that you took the time to research.

2. It also provides suggestions for further reading. I know that as a reader I have been very pleased to have just such a bibliography included, so that I can explore the historical period and the characters mentioned further.

CHAPTER SIX - After the first draft

Congratulations. You have done the hard work and written your first draft. Now, what do you do? Try to find an agent? Format it for self-publication?

No. You set it aside for a week or two, that's what.

You will no doubt be elated, if a little worn out, and want to plough on through with your book, but you need to have a break from it for a little while in order to see it objectively. Not looking at it for a few weeks will allow you to come back to your first draft with a refreshed brain and a clearer vision for your novel.

Starting the second draft

Your writing journey does not end with your first draft. Your first draft will be incomplete, almost certainly contain poor grammar, confused sections and wishy-washy dialogue. That's alright, it's supposed to. The second draft is where you put these things right.

You will have to be ruthless when you go through your manuscript. You will not only be correcting grammar and spelling, but editing. You may find that scene you thought was beautifully written just isn't necessary to the plot and actually holds the story up, so it has to come out. You might discover that you have skipped an important plot development and need to write some new scenes.

A common problem experienced by novice writers is the tendency to put in plenty of 'He said' and 'She said' into the dialogue. Often this is unnecessary, especially when the dialogue only involves two people and it is easy to tell who is talking. Another mistake is to use impressive-sounding words where a simple one will do or describe an action where it isn't necessary. For example, don't use "'My word!' he ejaculated", to describe how your character responds. The dialogue itself should give an indication of this.

Cliff-hangers are not just for thrillers. As you go through your first draft, check to make sure that all your chapters end with a hook to encourage the reader to carry on reading. This can be achieved by ending the chapter in the middle of the action, such as a character turning around as a door opens. Finish your chapter here, and continue the story in the next one by identifying the new arrival.

You may use the second draft to refine your story, and leave the fine-tuning editing and proofing for the third draft. This is how I prefer to work, and you might find that you do too.

A word of warning: you will know your story inside out, and it is very easy to make assumptions on behalf of your readers. For example, you may know that your character started off as a knight and was then ennobled to an earl and you've demonstrated that by changing the way he is addressed. However, your readers may think you've made a mistake if you don't include an exposition scene where his ennoblement is mentioned. Information such as this, while it is not inherently dramatic and therefore doesn't deserve a big mention, still needs to be included in some way to allow your readers to make the connection. Also, it may be obvious to you that Henry VIII's mother was Elizabeth of York, but don't assume that your readers know it too. People read historical novels because they have an interest in a certain period and enjoy learning about it. If you're lucky, your historical novel will whet the appetites of your readers to find out more about your characters and their world. Make sure it is as accurate, informative and tantalising as possible without turning it into a history book.

Nearing the end

So now you've completed a second draft, maybe even a third and you think your book is done. It's not perfect, but then, we writers are never entirely happy with what we've written, are we? We know it could always be better.

What to do with your manuscript now?

Years ago, if you were intent on publication, you would have to find a literary agent who would take you on and represent you to a publishing house. It was notoriously difficult to do, and writers would, without exception, have to cope with numerous rejections.

The publishing world has changed dramatically. Admittedly, there is an undeniable kudos to having a publishing house demonstrate faith in your work by agreeing to take you on, but this is no longer your only option. Self-publishing has now become the way to see your work in print. Even established authors have ditched their publishers to self-publish, preferring to receive the higher royalties that cutting out the middle man means. Also, I have heard that many publishing houses are notorious for doing very little to publicise their author's work, and that it is pretty much up to the author to do all the marketing themselves, so it may be that there are not many advantages to taking the traditional publishing route anymore.

Whatever you choose to do with your novel, I wish you good luck.

~

Turn the page to read the first chapter from my historical novel, *The Queen's Favourite*.

The Queen's Favourite

1

Greenwich Palace, London, February 1542

Robert Dudley was bored. Bored with the lesson, bored with Master Cheke droning on about Seneca, Suetonius and other long dead Romans. Bored with sitting still for hour upon hour.

He sighed and ran his fingers through his dark hair. If only the rest of his classmates felt the same, perhaps there could be a mutiny. He knew he would be able to count on his brothers, Ambrose, Henry and Guildford. Ambrose sat beside him, his chin cradled in one hand while the other idly swept away wood shavings from where he had scratched his name into his desk with his penknife. Robert could hear Henry and Guildford playing cards beneath their desk behind him. But he knew the others wouldn't dare. Not Prince Edward nor Jane Grey sitting, all attention, at the front of the class. Not Jane's sisters, neither; the tall and pretty Catherine, nor the freak of the family, the hunch-backed dwarf Mary, at the back where no one paid her any mind.

But maybe Elizabeth would be with him? She was sitting in front of Robert, head bent, scribbling furiously. She too was paying little heed to Master Cheke, not because of boredom, but because she had learnt this lesson months before in private study and had now moved on to the Ancient Greeks.

'Master Robert!'

Robert jerked his attention back to his tutor. 'Yes, Master Cheke?' he said, his lips broadening into a grin.

Charming though his smile was, it had little effect upon the old scholar. Cheke sighed as he leant on a pile of books. 'Master Robert, I realise that study of the Classics holds little interest for such an energetic boy as yourself, but your parents have arranged for you to be educated with the children of His Majesty the king, and you would do well to follow their example and attend to your books, instead of gazing around the room like a moonstruck calf. Do you comprehend me, sir?'

Robert bent his head in answer and dipped the tip of his quill into the inkpot, grinning as he heard Elizabeth snigger. Master Cheke, satisfied that Robert was behaving, turned his back and began to search through another pile of books heaped on a chest by the wall. Robert stole a look out of the window and saw that it had finally stopped raining. He leant forward and hissed at Elizabeth. When she turned her frowning face to him, he jerked his head towards the door. Her frown deepened disapprovingly and she shook her head. He glared at her, his black eyes insisting fiercely. She poked her tongue out at him and turned away. Robert eased his backside from the stool and groped around the desk. Ambrose opened bleary eyes to see what his brother was up to and watched in amusement as Robert grabbed Elizabeth's wrist, plucked the quill from between her fingers and tugged her from her stool. She grimaced, but allowed herself to be led from the schoolroom. Ambrose's gaze wandered to Master Cheke, who was wholly unaware that his star pupil and the mischief-maker had absconded. He closed his eyes, wondering how long it would take the tutor to realise.

'I wanted to work,' Elizabeth protested feebly as Robert pulled her along the corridors of the palace.

'It was boring.'

'Let go of me,' she said, shaking her wrist free. 'Where are we going?'

'To the stables, of course.' Now that Elizabeth wasn't holding him up, he broke into a run. Elizabeth followed, hitching her skirts up to her bony knees.

'Wait for me,' she demanded as they dodged between servants, but his legs were longer and he reached the stable yard before her.

Curving his body around the door, Robert breathed in the aroma of straw and animal, too long absent from his nostrils. He moved along the stalls, murmuring greetings to the horses as they pressed their noses into his outstretched palm.

Horseshoes, hanging from nails on the back of the door, clattered, signalling Elizabeth's arrival. 'I told you to wait.'

He smiled, not looking up. 'They've missed me.'

'Stupid animals.' Elizabeth snatched an apple from a bulging sack leaning against the wall. She rubbed it against her bodice before snapping off a bite.

'You'd miss me if you didn't see me for a week.'

'Would not.'

'Would.'

'No, I wouldn't,' she insisted, stomping past him and flinging herself on a bale of hay. He took the apple from her hand as she passed and held it to the mouth of Phoebe, his favourite horse, who began to munch contentedly.

'You're in a foul mood today,' he said. 'If you keep your face as sour as that, the wind will change and you'll stay that way.'

'Pig. Speak so to me again and...'

'You'll what?'

'I'll...I'll...'

'What will you do? Banish me to the Tower, cut off my -.' He suddenly realised what he was saying and spun round to face her.

Elizabeth's eyes had grown wide at his words and her hand flew to her mouth. 'Cut off your head,' she finished, her voice breaking.

He hurried to her side and put his arm around her shoulder.

'Katherine,' she whispered in explanation.

'I know,' he said. 'I shouldn't have said that. I'm such an ass.'

They both knew about Katherine Howard, the pretty girl who had caught the lustful eye of the king and married him, letting him believe that he was the first to enjoy her young body. To deceive a king, one who was vain and suspicious, was dangerous, but her charms were plentiful and she hoped that a lack of virginity in a bride could perhaps have been forgiven, that is if she ever dared to tell the king the truth. But she had grown complacent, so secure in the king's love for her that she began to take one of his gentlemen to her bed. She was young, after all, and wanted to hold a man's body that was slim and smooth, unlike the bloated mass of her husband. She and her lover had been discovered, and the king found he was not in a forgiving mood. Katherine's lover had already died for his crime. Katherine, it was said, practised for her own execution on a block delivered to her Tower prison.

'Why is my father doing this?' Elizabeth asked.

'You don't know?' Robert was surprised.

Elizabeth shook her head. 'I heard some of my women talking, but they stopped when they saw me. How has Katherine offended my father, Robin?'

'I can't say, Bess. My father said I wasn't to mention it.'

'Oh, Rob, if you know, tell me please.'

'All right, but you didn't hear it from me. She deceived the king with another man. She bedded Thomas Culpeper.'

'What does bedded mean?'

'Don't tell me you don't know?' he laughed. 'And you're supposed to be the clever one.'

'Don't laugh at me.' Her pale cheeks had flushed red.

'But if you don't know,' he said airily, 'I suppose I could tell you.'

'Tell me,' she insisted, her tears drying.

So he told her what it meant, and laughed even harder when she clamped her hands over her ears and told him to shut up, to stop lying, that it wasn't true, her parents had never done such a disgusting thing.

'It is true.'

'I'm never going to do that.'

'You'll have to when you marry.'

'I'm not going to marry.'

'Of course you will.'

'Will not.'

'Will.'

'Will not.'

'There you are!'

They jumped at the shrill voice. Elizabeth's governess, Katherine Ashley, stood in the doorway, her hands on her hips, glowering at them.

'Kat,' Elizabeth said, 'how long have you been there?'

'Is it for you to question me, my lady?' Katherine retorted, holding up her skirts and stepping into the stable. 'My word, I could hear the two of you clear across the yard. Squabbling like brats from the docksides. Why aren't you in the schoolroom? I should have known he would have something to do with it. Do that again, my lad,' Katherine shook a finger at Robert as he rolled his eyes, 'and I'll have you up before your father before you can shake a stick.'

'He wouldn't care,' Robert muttered, kicking at the ground.

'What did he say?' Katherine demanded.

'Nothing, Kat,' Elizabeth said quickly. 'Come, let us go.' She jumped down from the hay bale and moving swiftly, slid her hand into Katherine's. 'I'll see you tomorrow,' she promised Robert, pushing Katherine through the door.

'Fooling in the stable with a courtier's son,' he heard Katherine say as her charge led her away. 'Whatever would people say?'

His lips curled at her words. Young as he was, the Dudley family pride was strong in him. How dare she scorn him for being the son of a mere courtier? After all, what was her precious Elizabeth but a bastard daughter of the king? He at least was born on the right side of the blanket. And he wouldn't be just a courtier's son forever. No, his father would see to that. His father would become great, and Robert great with him. Let Mistress Ashley look down her nose at him then.

He opened a stall door and lifted a saddle from its post. Phoebe whinnied and stamped, like him, impatient to be outside.

'There now, my lovely,' he said, kissing her neck and holding his cheek against the warm flesh. 'You know I can do it, don't you?'

Want to read more?

Buy the book at Amazon.

About Laura Dowers

I work as a freelance proofreader and copywriter, and own Blue Laurel Services for Authors, dedicated to helping authors self-publish their books. I am a member of the Society for Editors and Proofreaders.

Please visit www.bluelaurelsfa.com if you want to self-publish.

For more information on my books, please visit my author site: http://la7297.wix.com/lauradowers .

Printed in Great Britain
by Amazon.co.uk, Ltd.,
Marston Gate.